Lincolnshire Tramways
In Camera

by David N. Robinson

QUOTES LIMITED of BUCKINGHAM

MCMXCI

Published by Quotes Limited
Buckingham, England

Typeset in Plantin by
Key Composition, Northampton, England

Pictures Lithographed by
South Midlands Lithoplates Limited, Luton, England

Printed by Busiprint Limited
Buckingham, England

Bound by Charles Letts Limited
Glasgow, Scotland

© David N. Robinson 1991

ISBN 0 86023 384 7

The first tramway in Lincolnshire, it would appear, was as early as 1813-15, to carry coal from the Grantham Canal to Belvoir Castle just over the county boundary. In 1871 a tramway scheme was proposed from Boston to Frieston Shore and along a pier to deep water; in the 1880s rural tramways were proposed from Brigg to Lincoln and from Alford to Skegness; nothing came of any of them. However, there were eventually four tramway systems in Lincolnshire: Grimsby/Cleethorpes 1881-1937, Lincoln 1882-1929, Alford & Sutton 1884-1889, and Grimsby & Immingham 1912-1961.

A scheme for horse trams in Grimsby was proposed by the Provincial Tramway Co in 1876. Three years later the Great Grimsby Street Tramways Co was formed, with three miles of standard gauge line from Bargate to Park Street on the Cleethorpes boundary, where there was a depôt to stable 60 horses, and with a branch line along Freeman Street to Hainton Avenue. The service opened with eight horse trams on 4 June 1881; fare 2d for any distance. The tramway was extended into Cleethorpes to Poplar Road, opened 21 May 1887, with further extensions to Albert Road (1898), to Brighton Street and finally to Kingsway, when the new sea wall and promenade were completed in 1906. In 1890 a total of 1,008,697 passengers was carried, with a revenue of £6,055 against expenditure of £3,996 — clearly a profitable enterprise. By 1899 there were over 1.7 million passengers.

Grimsby and Cleethorpes began discussing electrification in 1897, an Electric Tramways Committee was formed, and the Provincial Tramway Co paid Cleethorpes £2,500 to widen Grimsby Road to take a double track. A new depôt was built at Pelham Road with its own electricity generating station. At 6.15am on Saturday 7 December 1901 driver Clements took the first electric tram from Pelham Road to Park Street, but could not proceed further until Grimsby switched on its power! In 1902 the fare from Brighton Street to People's Park

was 2½d for four miles, and weekly profit per car was £4 8s 6d. The £100,000 investment paid off as the number of passengers rose to 5 million by 1903.

To run the new service, 24 electric tramcars were bought from Dick, Kerr & Co (double-deck, open-top, each seating 56), and four second-hand single-deckers from the Alexandra Park Electric Railway, and some of the old horse-cars were rebuilt. By 1913 the number of passengers carried was 10 million, with the busiest section in Cleethorpes. Trams running in Cleethorpes were operated by the GGST, although after 1902 Cleethorpes could supply trams themselves. During the Great War services ceased at dusk in case the flashes from the overhead connections attracted Zeppelins.

In 1921 Grimsby Corporation bought the GGST for £104,143 and found the undertaking delapidated with cars poorly maintained. By 1925 the takeover was complete, a new depôt was built on Victoria Street using a World War I hangar from the Killingholme seaplane base, and the Welholme Road section and the Freeman Street branch line were abandoned. Sixteen second-hand Brush Electric flat-top double-deckers were bought from Sunderland District Tramways, and in 1929 Cleethorpes acquired 12 Brush Electric open-top double-deckers from the abandoned Gosport & Fareham Tramway.

Cleethorpes paid £50,000 to the undertaking to create Cleethorpes Corporation Transport and took over their section of the Line (Kingsway to Park Street) on 2 July 1936, with a fleet of 26 tramcars. In November the same year Grimsby ceased running trams and changed to trolleybuses. Cleethorpes continued with trams for seven months until the closing trip on 17 July 1937.

The Lincon Tramways Co was formed in 1882, and a single track line with passing loops was laid from St Benedict's

Square to the Gate House Hotel in Bracebridge where a depôt and stables were built. The service began the following year; journey time was 20 minutes and the fare 2d. By 1903 the company had ten cars and 24 horses and carried a million passengers. A year later Lincoln Coporation took over the company for £10,488. On 22 July 1905 the horse cars were withdrawn and waggonettes provided a service, until the Griffith-Bedell Surface Contact Electrical System could be installed in the road between the tram lines.

By this system, the first of its kind in the country, power was supplied from metal studs in the road to a magnetic skate under the trams. There were eight trams, open-top double-deckers, seating 58 and made by Brush Electrical. After a trial run on Sunday 29 October, the line was officially opened on 23 November 1905. There were plans for extensions east and west in 1913, but not implemented because of the war. In 1915 the line was carrying 1½ million passengers, with a tram every six minutes on weekdays and Saturdays. The stud system was never entirely satisfactory and in 1919 was replaced by overhead power lines. The first motor omnibuses appeared in 1920, and the tramway was closed on 4 March 1929.

The Alford & Sutton steam tramway was shortlived. Proposed in 1880, it opened on 2 April 1884 and cost more than £30,000. Just over eight miles in length, the 2ft 6ins gauge line followed the road across the Marsh through Bilsby, Markby and Hannah, and was licensed to carry freight as well as passengers. The line had three steam locomotives, five passenger cars and a number of goods wagons. There were two services each way on weekdays and Saturdays, return fare 1s (children 6d). Following opening of the Willoughby & Sutton branch railway in 1886, receipts declined rapidly and the tramway ceased running in December 1889.

The Grimsby & Immingham Electric Railway was built by the Great Central Railway, contracted to R. W. Blackwell & Co for the street section from Corporation Bridge to Pyewipe (£16,474) where a small depôt was built, and to Price, Wills & Reeve for the country section (£11,360). Power for the six-mile single track line was from the generating station on Immingham Dock, with electrical equipment by Dick, Kerr & Co. The tramway opened on 15 May 1912, and was soon extended with double track from Queen's Road, Immingham onto the dock estate (opened 17 November 1913). The service started with four 78-seater and four 48-seater bogie cars by Brush Electrical; four more long cars were added in 1913 and a further four in 1915; the short cars were withdrawn in 1930. Three cars with upholstered seats were bought from Newcastle on Tyne Corporation in 1948, but withdrawn in 1952 a year after 19 cars (48-seaters) were acquired from Gateshead & District Tramways.

The first service from Corporation Bridge was 5.10am, with three more cars at five minute intervals, then hourly to 7.15pm. From Immingham Dock the first car was 5.45am and hourly to 7.45pm, with the three extra cars from the morning returning between 5.30 and 6.30pm. The run took 20 minutes, fare 5d. By 1935 the cheap day return was 1s and the workman's return 7½d. During the severe winter of 1947 trams were the only vehicles to get through to Immingham for several days.

In June 1956 Grimsby Corporation bought and closed the street section and the terminus moved to Cleveland Bridge; 800,000 passengers a year were being carried. Three years later the peak time services were reduced, and working ceased on 1 July 1961. 'The Clickety', as it was affectionately known for its shake, rattle and roll ride, was the last Lincolnshire tramway.

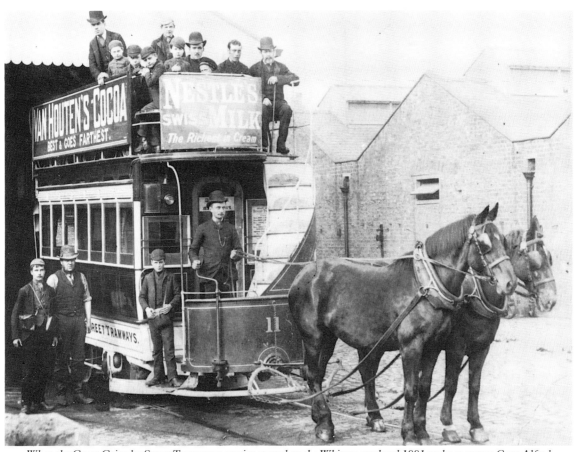

When the Great Grimsby Street Tramways service started on the Whitsun weekend 1881 under manager Capt Alfred Montenaro, there were eight horse-drawn cars, with others soon added because of their popularity. Here is Car 11 at the Park Street Depôt in the 1890s. The fare was 2d for any distance.

The tramway was extended from Park Street to Poplar Road in Cleethorpes in May 1887. Over a million passengers were carried in 1890, the date of this photograph. For a working day of 8am to 10.30pm a tram driver was paid 22s 6d a week, paid in pennies on Saturday night.

A horse-drawn tram waits on the passing loop in Victoria Street near the corner of West St Mary's Gate, and is photographed from the open top of a tram coming from the Old Market Place. After electrification in 1901 some of the horse-drawn trams were kept for use as trailers, mainly for football crowd traffic, and later sold to Lincoln Corporation, or were converted to electric cars.

Victoria Street just before the Great War; approaching the Riverhead is one of the cars made by Dick, Kerr & Co of Preston, originally open-topped and later fitted with a bowed top. On the left is Lawson & Stockdale, tailors, clothiers and outfitters, and on the right beyond the shops is the main post office.

Car 22 approaches the Riverhead along Victoria Street. On the left the National Provincial Bank is on the corner of New Street. To the right is South Dock Street (to Blow's Hull Steamers) with wall advertisements for Skelton's, noted for jackets and dresses at lowest cash prices, and M. Kitching, hay, straw, corn and potato merchant.

A JAY-EM-JAY series postcard of William Marshall & Sons' Victoria Mills, between Victoria Street and Alexandra Dock; curiously, when the artist included the two trams in the foreground he forgot to put in the overhead power lines (or perhaps the horses?)!

Car 39 on Cleethorpe Road, waiting at the railway crossing to the Docks, c1930. This was a prototype, built in 1925 in Cleethorpes (see pages 28 and 38), with the roof added later. (JHM)

Passengers boarding Car 4 at Riby Square in 1904; the B on the front indicated the service was to Bargate — the service had been extended over Deansgate Bridge to the Wheatsheaf in Bargate in 1901. The canopy advertisements are for Hudson's Soap and Huckett's Hats. The branch line turns into Freeman Street on the right. To the left is the bank of Smith Ellison and Co (later National Provincial).

Car 31 (now Grimsby Corporation Transport) passing through Riby Square on the way to the Old Market in the later 1920s; this car had been horse-drawn, was rebuilt by Dick, Kerr & Co as an open-top electric and the roof added later. It was acquired from Cleethorpes when Grimsby Corporation bought the Great Grimsby Street Tramways in 1925 and ran a joint service to Cleethorpes.

The tramway branch along Freeman Street and Hainton Street (now Avenue) was from Riby Square to Tasburgh Street (later extended to Welholme Road) and laid by Riggall & Hewins. The horse-drawn tram of the 1890s is outside the Prince of Wales Theatre in Freeman Street, rebuilt in 1866 in the Italianate style to seat 2,500.

The Great Grimsby Street Tramways service on Freeman Street c1920, with Car 2 and an open-top near the passing loop by the Market; the Prince of Wales Theatre (right) advertises 'The Thief', and on the corner of Duncombe Street (left) is George Munning's bar. Beyond is the spire of St Andrew's, the fishermen's church, and the Dock Tower.

The passing loop was on the bend of Hainton Avenue, with Car 2 approaching the branch line terminus in the residential area of Grimsby. The open balcony at front and rear had a curved seat for three. Standards for the overhead lines are on the left side of the road.

The tram service along the Freeman Street/Hainton Avenue branch line ceased in 1926, because of the cost of replacing the track, and Grimsby Corporation introduced the Garrett trolleybus; they cost £1,475 each. Here No 1 approaches Riby Square.

Car 18 of the Great Grimsby Street Tramways travelling along Cleethorpe Road from Riby Square towards Cleethorpes, was one of 24 cars built by Dick, Kerr & Co in 1901; in the lower compartment there were longitudinal seats for 30, and seats with swing-over backs accommodated 26 on the upper deck. The livery was green (lined in gold and white) and cream (lined in black and red). Standards for the overhead power lines are in the centre of the road. The large shop on the right is Bon Marché, advertising curtains, carpets and bedsteads on the blinds.

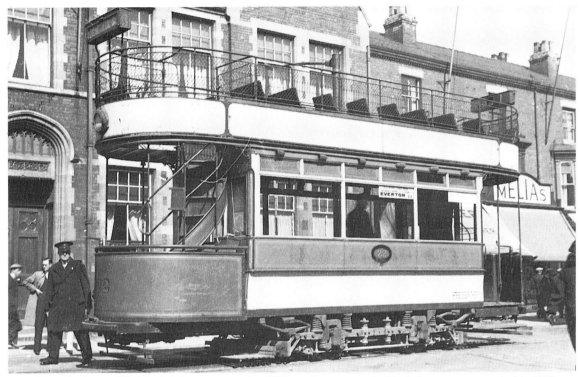

When Cleethorpes UDC had their own trams after 1925, twelve open-top double-decker cars were acquired in 1929 from the abandoned Gosport & Fareham Tramway. In 1935/36 Cleethorpes paid £50,000 to create Cleethorpes Corporation Transport (Manager F. H. Peacock) with a total of 26 cars. Here is No 22 outside Clee Park Hotel on the boundary with Grimsby, in April 1937. On the window is a handbill for a First Division football match at Blundell Park, Grimsby Town v Everton. (HBP)

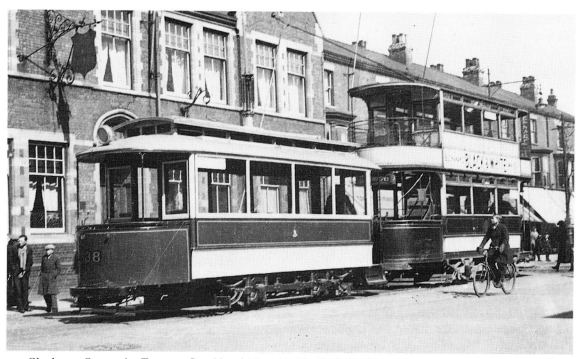

Cleethorpes Corporation Transport Cars 38 and 43 outside Clee Park Hotel in April 1937; single-decker No 38 had been acquired from Southport and was distinctive in having a clerestory roof. It was used mainly for advertisements and illuminations; it would be the last tram to run (see page 41). Flat-topped double-decker No 43 (made by Brush Electric) was one of two ex-Sunderland District Tramway cars acquired from Grimsby in 1925, but retaining the Grimsby livery. (HBP)

They were changing the poles on three trams near the Park Street boundary (Clee Park Hotel in the background) on Saturday 24 April 1937, probably in readiness for the home football match with Everton, as the destination boards show Blundell Street. Nos 28 and 22 are ex-Gosport & Fareham open-top double-deckers, with ex-Southport No 38 single-decker between. (HBP)

Car No 40 was built in 1921 as an open-top tourer for use in the summer only. Seen here outside the gates of People's Park, at the terminus of the extension from Bargate, it ran 6d trips to Cleethorpes. It was withdrawn after only three seasons and transferred to the Portsdown & Horndean Light Railway.

The leafy approach to Deansgate Bridge from Bargate, with open-top car 21 approaching; in the background is St James' church.

Two electric trams mix with horse traffic at the corner of the Old Market Place, leading to Deansgate Bridge beyond. In front of St James' church is the unusually worded wall sign of the firm J. H. TURNER, DRAPER Etc.

Car 16 (B for Bargate service) passes through the Old Market Place from Bethlehem Street. It was one of the original 24 cars on Brill 21E trucks supplied by Dick, Kerr & Co in 1901. On the left, the cart of S. T. Lancaster, coal and coke dealer, follows the tram lines round the Corn Exchange.

The Corn Exchange is seen here from the Victoria Street side of the Old Market Place, just before the Great War, with Car 37 approaching. This bow-topped double-decker was exhibited at a tramway exihibition in 1908.

Leaving the Old Market Place towards Bargate about 1930 (the extension to Welholme Road having been abandoned in 1926) is Grimsby Corporation Tramways No 34. This had been a horse-drawn tram and was rebuilt by Dick, Kerr & Co. (SLS)

OPPOSITE: *When electrification arrived in 1901, the Great Grimsby Street Tramways built a new depôt in Pelham Road, Cleethorpes with its own electricity generating station. It also had workshops to design and build trams; eight were built from 1925-28. Car 39 was the prototype, seen here as new in July 1925.*

ABOVE: Double-decker 28 and single-decker 38 of Cleethorpes Corporation Transport stand outside the Pelham Road Depôt in April 1937. The depôt had eight sheds 186ft long to accommodate 40 cars.

The interior of the Pelham Road Depôt in June 1935 contained three double-decker cars of Great Grimsby Street Tramways; the one at the back is jacked up for inspection and perhaps repair.

Car 59, travelling along Alexandra Road, Cleethorpes towards the Kingsway about 1930, was one of the last to be built in the Pelham Road workshops. On the right is the Empire Cinematograph Theatre (former Music Hall).

Alexandra Road about 1906, with open-top double-decker Car 12 approaching; access to the finely decorated iron balconies above the shops gave sea views across the fenced gardens (right). Below you could enjoy The Old Original Oysters purveyed by Samuel Knowles or dinner at the refreshment rooms of Mrs Hannah Flinders.

Approaching High Cliff, Cleethorpes along Alexandra Road is bow-topped Car 29, built as an open-top by Dick, Kerr & Co in 1901 and covered in 1925. On the left, Car 6 going towards Grimsby had a similar history. On the right is the turnstile entrance to the Pier Gardens.

Car 28 was dressed overall for the opening of the Kingsway in Cleethorpes by Lady Henderson on 12 July 1906, after she had cut the first sod of Immingham Dock earlier in the day. The Kingsway promenade had been built under the Cleethorpes Improvement Act 1902 and enabled the terminus to be moved from Brighton Street. The number panel on this car says the Provincial Tramways Company, who put up the original scheme in the 1870s, but it would appear that the car was built in Germany as a single-decker and formerly used on the Alexandra Park Electric Railway in North London before being rebuilt as an open-top double-decker.

An afternoon stroll on the Kingsway, with a calm high tide, about 1910: the tram standing at the terminus (right) is No 23 or 24; these were unique in being fitted with Whites Top Covers — fully glazed balconies and a clerestory roof.

Car 22 at the Kingsway terminus on 25 June 1933 had been acquired from the abandoned Gosport & Fareham tramway in 1929. Note that the destination is Park Street on the Cleethorpes/Grimsby boundary. (MJO)

Looking along the Kingsway Gardens towards the tramway terminus about 1925, in the foreground are the stocks, once in Cuttleby mid-way between the two hamlets of Oole and Itterby, which became part of Cleethorpes. In the background is the full length pier with its two pavilions.

Car 39 at the Kingsway terminus was the prototype open-top later fitted with a roof (see pages 11 and 28), and carrying advertisements for Albert Gait, bookseller, stationer and printer (still in business today) and Burgon's Stores (in Freeman Street) — Grimsby's Grocer for Breakfast Bacon. (HAW)

Car 47 at the Kingsway terminus on 15 June 1935, originally one of the open-balcony cars built by Brush Electric, was bought from Sunderland District Electric Tramways. When Cleethorpes took over their section of the undertaking in July 1936, this was one of the cars transferred from Grimsby Corporation Tramways while retaining the Grimsby livery.

One of the first horse-drawn trams (No 10) stands at the Albert Road terminus on Alexandra Road in 1890. The track had been extended from Poplar Road and along High Street in Cleethorpes. This involved ascending Isaac's Hill where the assistance of a third horse was required.

The end of the line: Goodbye Old Faithful — Grimsby had ceased running trams in November 1936, but Cleethorpes continued for a few more months. On the night of Saturday 17 July 1937, Car 38, suitably draped and illuminated and with local dignitaries aboard, left the Kingsway terminus on the final run. On the left is the Queen Victoria Jubilee Fountain.

This is one of the earliest pictures of a horse-drawn tram in Lincoln, at the High Street terminus by St Benedict's Square, in 1903. The Lincoln Tramways Company was formed in 1882 with a fleet of eight horse-drawn trams operating from St Benedict's Square to the Gate House Hotel, Bracebridge. The journey took 20 minutes and the fare was 2d. This tram has just arrived and the horse is being brought round to start the journey to Bracebridge.

'To Memory Dear' this photograph was captioned — the last journey of Lincoln horse-drawn trams on Saturday 22 July 1905, seen here by the Midland Railway (St Marks) level crossing on the High Street.

* Mr. GEORGE PIMP the Driver of the FIRST CAR in 1882,
the LAST CAR on 22nd July, 1905.

In Affectionate Remembrance

OF THE

LINCOLN HORSE CARS

which succumbed to an Electric Shock, after years of faithful service,
22nd July, 1905.

"GONE BUT NOT FORGOTTEN."

'Gone but not forgotten': this special postcard was brought out to mark the end of the Lincoln horse cars, and perhaps the 23-year service of George Pimp. Lincoln Corporation had taken over the Tramways Company in 1904 and made plans to have electric trams.

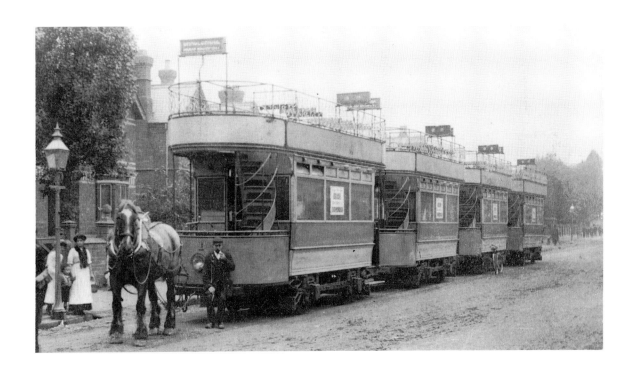

These are the first four of eight open-top double-decker trams being delivered to the tram sheds on Newark Road, Bracebridge, photographed near where is now the Smith's Crisps factory. They were made by Brush Electrical Engineering at Loughborough, at a cost of £600 each, and could seat 58 passengers.

The trial run of the first electric tramcar (No 6) in Lincoln, on Sunday 29 October 1905, attracted a lot of photographic attention. Behind is the Bracebridge Depôt, being altered to accommodate the double-decker cars.

This was taken at the same time as the photograph opposite, probably near the tramsheds on Newark Road, Bracebridge. Some of the same onlookers appear in both, and the children had difficulty in standing still for the long exposure photograph. The seating on the upper deck had swing backs to allow passengers to face the direction of travel.

The Lincoln trial run was a crowd-puller along Newark Road, and Car 6, now with 'Engaged Car' on the destination board, had taken on board those privileged to try it out, presumably members of the Corporation.

Another group posed for the trial run in October 1905. The power was taken up from studs set slightly below road level between the tram lines. It was the GB Surface Contact Electric Tramway system, invented by B. H. Bedell, and in Lincoln was the first of its type to operate in this country. The break in service between the last horse tram in July and the first electric tram was to allow for installation of the system in the road.

The official opening of the Lincoln Electric Tramway on Thursday 23 November 1905 was a day of excitement, although from this photograph it appears to have been an all-male affair. The Black Bull Hotel (left) on High Street was jus below the terminus at St Benedict's Square.

The other official photograph was at the Bracebridge terminus, outside the Gate House Hotel (right), when at least some ladies (and babies) were there to see the first decorated tram arrive. Electrification reduced the travel time on the full route to 15 minutes.

Looking up High Street, Lincoln one morning about 1908, Car 6 passes the Cornhill (right), with Hepworth, clothier and outfitters on the corner. The track was single, with passing loops, and there was a tram every six minutes on weekdays and Saturdays. The fare from St Benedict's Square to the Gate House Hotel, Bracebridge was ½d.

The photographer stood at almost exactly the same place one sunny afternoon (the shadows are now to the right) about the same year, with Car 2 on the way to St Benedict's Square. The power studs in the road between the tram lines can just be seen. Next to the Queen Hotel on the right is the shop of Charles Keyworth, printer, advertising picture postcards, guides and views of Lincoln, where this postcard could have been bought.

City of Lincoln Tramways Car 6 in 1910 had the upper decks of the fleet enclosed to give a glazed compartment but with open balconies under a flat roof. The shop on the left is C. Pepperdine, Fancy Repository, 412 High Street — on the east side between Pennell Street and Queen Street.

The system of taking power from studs in the road was never entirely satisfactory and was replaced by overhead power lines in 1919. Here Car 7 passes the turning to Cross O'Cliff Hill on its way to Bracebridge. The last tram ran at 3.30pm on Monday 4 March 1929, and motor 'buses took over.

Alford Market Place on the afternoon of Wednesday 2 April 1884 witnessed the opening of the Alford & Sutton Steam Tramway. The carriage was packed, with people standing in the open balconies at each end, and seats had also been provided in the goods truck. The steam tram locomotive is No 2, built that year by Merryweather & Sons of Greenwich. The 2ft 6ins gauge tram lines along the road across the Marsh through Bilsby, Markby and Hannah had been laid by the Scottish firm W. B. Dick & Co.

A mixed train of goods wagons and a passenger car at the Station Road terminus of the tramway in Alford, was hauled by locomotive No 1, with its distinctively tall ornamental chimney; it was built in 1883 by Black, Hawthorne & Co of Gateshead, and had been used for hauling materials in the construction of the tramway.

DICK, KERR & CO.,

101, LEADENHALL STREET, LONDON, E.C.

𝔚𝔬𝔯𝔨𝔰:—BRITANNIA ENGINEERING WORKS. KILMARNOCK, N.B.

SOLE MAKERS OF MORRISON & KERR'S PATENT TRAMWAY ENGINES

AS SUPPLIED TO THE ALFORD AND SUTTON AND NORTH LONDON STEAM TRAMWAYS.

PRICES AND FULL PARTICULARS ON APPLICATION.

MAKERS OF ALL CLASSES OF CARS & ROLLING STOCK FOR STREET TRAMWAYS & NARROW GAUGE RAILWAYS.

Locomotive No 3, built for the tramway by Dick, Kerr & Co (successors to W. B. Dick & Co) in 1885, featured on one of the firm's advertisements. The firm almost certainly made some of the passenger cars used on the line.

The other terminus of the steam tramway was at the sea end of High Street in the seaside resort of Sutton le Marsh (as it then was). The white building on the right is the Jolly Bacchus Hotel but, curiously on this illustration, the run-around loop is missing. Following opening of the Willoughby and Sutton railway in 1886, and joining up with the Louth-Mablethorpe branch line two years later, the Alford & Sutton Tramway only lasted until 15 November 1889, when the undertaking was wound up.

The Grimsby & Immingham Electric Railway was built by the Great Central Railway Company, running 5⅜ miles from Corporation Bridge in Grimsby to Queen's Road, Immingham, and opened on Sunday 12 May 1912. This is one of the first four 54ft 2ins bogie cars, each seating 64 passengers in two compartments (smoking and non-smoking) on wooden strip seats with swing backs; there were also eight tip-up seats in the central luggage compartment (a favourite place for daily card gambling). They were made by the Brush Electrical Engineering Co, Loughborough, who supplied four more in 1913 and a further four in 1915, as well as four shorter 48-seaters when the line opened.

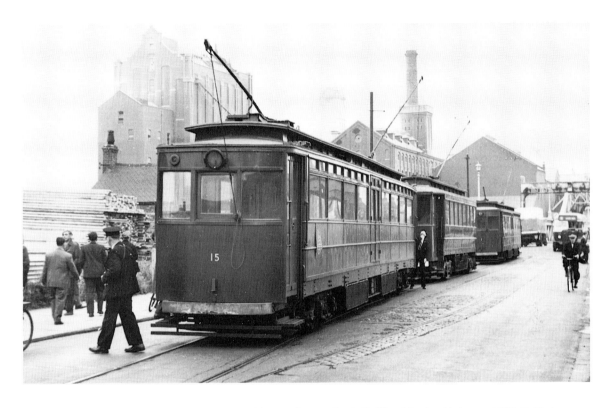

Cars 15, 33 and 3 wait at the Corporation Bridge terminus on Bank Holiday Monday 28 August 1955. Behind on the other side of Alexandra Dock are the Victoria Flour Mills.

Car 33 was one of a batch of 18 bought from Gateshead & District Tramways in 1951; this one was built by Brush Electrical. Left is the waiting room and parcels office; on a normal working day there would be enormous stacks of bicycles by the Tramway Station left by men who worked in Immingham.

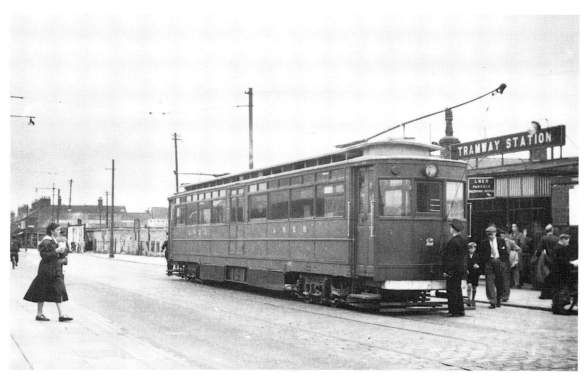

Monday 21 August 1950 was a normal working day, but most of the traffic was early morning and evening. Still bearing the letters LNER, Car 2 changes poles at the Corporation Bridge terminus; it was withdrawn from service the following year. Maximum speed for trams on the street section was 12mph. (RPB)

On Sunday 10 June 1956, Car 4 approaches the passing loop at Beeson Street on Corporation Road, hence the road sign TRAM PINCH because of the narrowing space available for other traffic. On the left is the Duke of York (or Boulevard) Gardens.

Gilbey Road crossed the railway by Cleveland Bridge (known locally as The Tip). Car 31 (ex-Gateshead), crosses the bridge on the way to Immingham on the enthusiasts' excursion of Sunday 10 June 1956, with some of them hurrying to board again after a photo stop. This was the last month of operation of the Grimsby street section, and the terminus was moved to the other side of Cleveland Bridge on 1 July (and the accompanying stacks of bicycles every working day).

Car 12 on the June 1956 excursion turns off Gilbey Road onto the Pyewipe section of the line, past the sign warning motorists not to overtake trams on the bridge.

The sidings at the Pyewipe Depôt full of trams; this was the day after the disastrous East Coast Flood of 31 January 1953 which caused damage and flooding along the Humber Bank. Cars at the front are (L-R): No 26 — bought from Gateshead & District Tramways in 1951 (made in Gateshead in 1920s); No 12 and No 1 — two of the original long cars (built 1913 and 1912); No 6 — one of three cars bought from Newcastle on Tyne Corporation in 1948. (JHM)

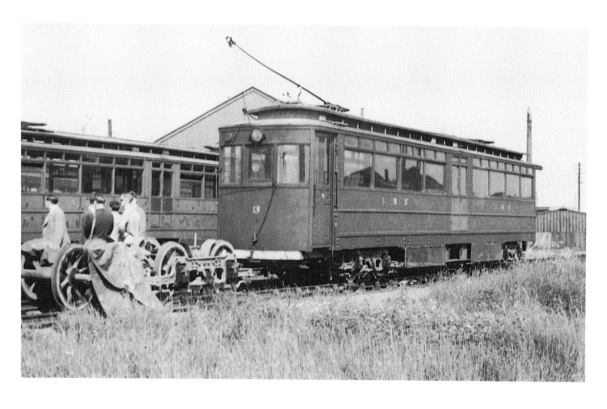

At the Pyewipe Depôt on Sunday 4 June 1950, Car 3 looks in need of a repaint; perhaps that is happening to one of the original cars behind which has been taken off the bogies (foreground). (RBP)

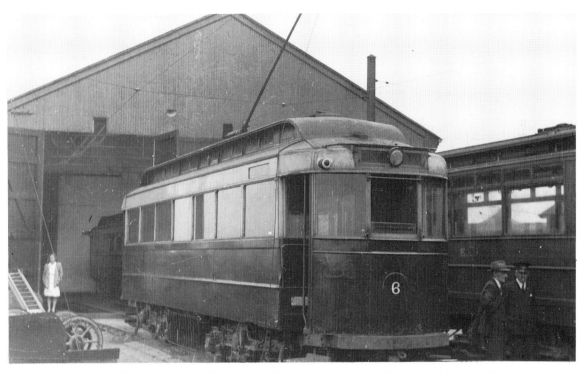

Car 6 newly arrived from Newcastle in August 1948, bought with two others. They were originally built in 1901, and rebuilt 1932-33, with 40 upholstered seats in one compartment. They were the only upholstered cars on the tramway, but were withdrawn in 1952. Behind is the small Pyewipes Depôt with only three workshops, so most of the cars were always out of doors. (JHM)

Car 30 (ex-Gateshead) in British Rail livery was unusually photographed next to a 2-8.0 steam locomotive in November 1955. It shows clearly the different sized wheels on the bogie of the team. When the services at peak times were reduced in 1959, many of the 18 ex-Gateshead cars like this one were laid up for long periods. (RBP)

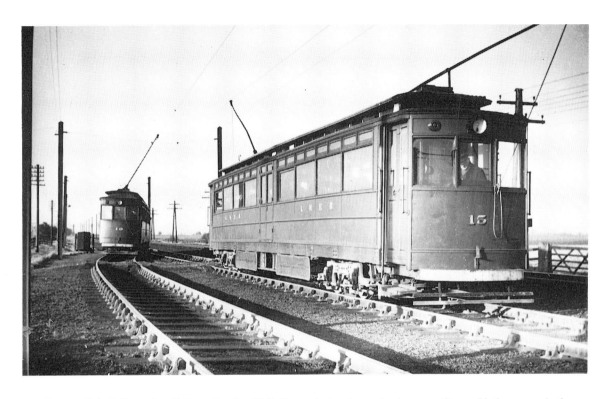

Low sunlight in December 1946 catches Car 10 (left) negotiating the passing loop near Courtaulds factory out in the country on the way to Immingham, as Car 15 waits to proceed to Grimsby. Car 10 was withdrawn from service in 1951. (RBP)

Excursion day 1955 at the Immingham Town reversing loop on Queen's Road; the double track extension over the bridge behind (opened November 1913) led to the terminus on Immingham Dock. The power lines are carried on concrete 'Cleopatra needles' on either side of the road. In front is the ex-Gateshead car, bought in 1951, which was converted to a repair car, with extending tower wagon for access to overhead power lines.

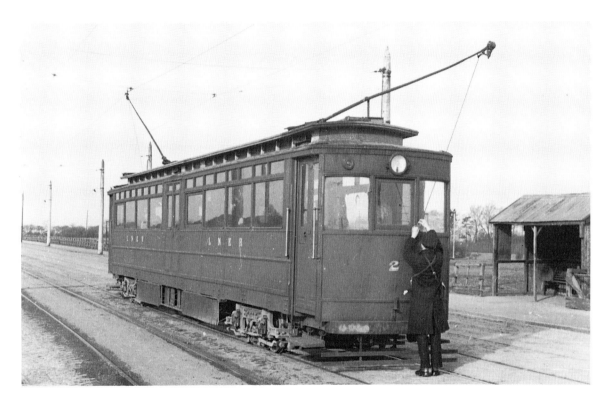

Original GCR Car No 2 changes poles at the Immingham 'Town' reversing halt on Queen's Road, 1949. It was withdrawn from service two years later. Note the rudimentary passenger shelter on the right.

Immingham Dock.

An early aerial impression of Immingham Dock, used for publicity, shows lots of activity. The tramway to carry workmen was completed two months before the dock opened; the terminus, as yet without a building, is to the left of the open lock gate.

Another publicity postcard produced by the Great Central Railway at the opening of Immingham Dock in July 1912 shows the graving dock left, and a tram just left of the three-storey dock offices.

Ex-Gateshead Car 26, in BR livery, by the East Jetty at Immingham Dock terminus awaits departure for Grimsby. This car was made in the late 1920s and seated 48 passengers. Note the different size of wheels on the bogies. (DT)

The Tramway Station terminus on Immingham Dock near the lock gates; it was opened in 1913 and is seen here in 1939 with GCR long cars 11 (built 1913) and 13 (built 1915). The power station which generated electricity for the line was on the other side of the lock gates (the chimney is between the two power poles behind the left tram), transmitting through three substations.

GCR Car 15 (built 1915), with photographers in the front cab, approaches the Kiln Lane, Stallingborough road crossing on its last run on Saturday 1 July 1961. The fare on the last day was 2s 1d return. (RBP)

The convoy of six cars on the last service of the Grimsby-Immingham Electric Railway was led by GCR Car 4 (built by Brush Electric in 1912), passing the sidings of redundant cars at the Pyewipe Depôt. There the cars were stripped and burned. Of the original GCR cars, only No 14 (built 1915) survives — in a shed at Crich. (RBP)

Index to Illustrations

Key to Photographers

(where identified)

DT	D. Tate	MJO	M. J. O'Connor
HAW	H. A. Whitcombe	RBP	R. B. Parr
HBP	H. B. Priestley	SLS	S. L. Smith
	JHM	J. H. Meredith	

All photographs are from the author's collection.